PHOENIX *Suites*

Sor Ausan –

Shank you for including
me in your series.
AND – thank you
for the trade!
cheers.

PHOENIX *Suites*

Miles Waggener

2002 WASHINGTON PRIZE *winner*

THE WORD WORKS
WASHINGTON, D.C.

The WORD WORKS
PO Box 42164
Washington, DC 20015
editor@wordworksdc.com

Cover Art: Matt Hamon
"Natasha With Sea Gull" 1999
Gelatin Silver Print, 14 in. x 14 in.

Matt Hamon
"Noah With Robin" 1999
Gelatin Silver Print, 14 in. x 14 in.

Both images ©Matt Hamon.

Book design, typography by Janice Olson.

Library of Congress Number: 2002115055
International Standard Book Number: 0-915380-52-8

ACKNOWLEDGMENTS

Grateful acknowledgment is made to the editors of the following publications, in which some of these poems, some in different versions, appeared: *Alligator Juniper:* "Looking for Federico"; *Beacon Street Review:* "Tides" (published as "When the Water Leaves"); *The Laurel Review:* "Harvest" (published as "My Father's Harvest"); *Mid-American Review:* "Quail"; *Puerto del Sol:* "Sleepers"; *Sonora Review:* "Roils" (published as "What New Roils"); *Willow Springs:* "Antonio Machado and the Trees."

Thank you to Bob Baker, Chris Dombrowski, Meg Gannon, Patricia Goedicke, James Jay, Joanna Klink, Greg Pape, and Jim Simmerman.

for Meg

Contents

Ringing under the stars we walked
To where it would have wet our feet
Had it been water.

George Oppen

Sand
you demand in return,
for the last
rose back at home
this evening also wants to be fed
out of the trickling hour.

Paul Celan

Direction

Here are landmarks
    and if you should find
        the magician's tomb
    the Sinagua built
in the maze
    of cinder cones and scrub
        keep quiet about it.
    Skeletons and talismans
are in boxes in Washington.
    Only you would want to know
        the way to a robbed grave.
    Find a slow chain
of rail cars pushing on
    beyond withering
        tennis courts and follow
    clattering shadows
and graffiti
    through town
        past curio shops
    live bait and ammo
the Napa Auto
    the Mormon church
        and reach
    a frontage road.
Take it as far east
    as you can—power
        lines humming overhead
    ponderosas and junipers
dwindling to salt bush—
    until the sun ends
        and a gas lamp appears
    in the clouded window
of a derelict school bus.
    The man selling
        ersatz Kachina dolls
    will tell you
he is your last landmark.

Valley

Traffic: a line across a dam, lightning, glimpses of architecture,
of rock, swollen
water on passenger side, on driver side a trickle in the canyon's
throat running
at our back, reaching the city cavernous with lights, with pools:
ants descending
amphitheater steps: the harbinger: a dead owl on cracked salt
flats: what watched us
for so long is a cup of sandy wind: trapped sound: a traveling
hymn through
a socket that we flood, that we climb out of tonight, but just to
speak of it sends
our tongues sinking wheel-ward in a mire: crossing double yellow
lines you are
lifting your blouse to be headless, to show the screamers in
limousines who
are also naked, now threading brake lights away from us to a more
ripening center:
a flame maybe water spouting stories high where we are reenacted
nightly: ground or
pardon, zero if a watcher were here to smile on us, do not rely on
your own understanding
yet: after hours, the host ushers us through a gauzy chamber:
lavender dregs of
a candle gutter inside what has to be a dog's skull: what has become:
we are home inside it.

HEAT

Because it
is never jealous,
never tired,
does not judge
and drinks more deeply
than we do
from shallow reservoirs,
because it is
ecumenical and lifts
plastic bags as willingly
as the hawk
bewildered above us,
perhaps because it
gathers around
dry-cleaner fires
and the orphanage as much
as the bullet
inside the coughing
mute's head,
and is found inside pills
as well as inside
my friend who has
just taken the pills,
somewhere
off this interstate
where light
strides slowly
across carpet…
Perhaps because it is within
his power and within
peeling billboard hands
cradling a billboard

infant on Alma School Road
riding the only bus
running this late—
which now burns
gears and oil
to climb an onramp
toward hospital lights
and shopping cart
on the shoulder,
past helicopters
catching their breath
above a stillborn
gunman's van—
one palm tree
has given up and bows
its head toward
the small plot of oasis
from which it grew.

PHOENIX SUITES

I.

Consider the tired horses in the Salt River Valley, their last legs
falling through grass as high as a Spanish bridle.

Our fathers' prayers and songs spun over the waters are lost;
the desert has devoured them like old ball courts and beetle-

polished bones. Cicadas grow louder in the hills surrounding
the house. Like coyote or worry, it could be a lone singer or

a swarm. What has the helicopter found to make it scour
the same stretch of Indian School Road—the engine and light

crashing through the palms. A construction worker finds
a shell the Hohokam patterned with bands, villages inside

valleys, desert worlds inside worlds. Forgotten lines travel inside
his palm. Is there something old in us that wants to dig holes

and fill them? To attract the dead, dig a trench on the lawn,
fill it with oxblood and mescal. I don't know where I'm from—

a flood plain, a warning, a family tree, the lines in my
grandfather's hands. And the shells testify to this.

II.

I've taken out a map to consider where on the Verde River
the divers found the hermit's body. On his desk, spider webs,

an old mask, the hemisphere of a face. The Central Arizona Project,
the canal, the water gossamer Phoenix hangs by, is hemmed in

with chain link warnings: no swimming, no fishing, patrolled by
aircraft. Camping by the old mines, I am startled out of my bag to

grope for my glasses. Wild donkeys, descendants of failed endeavor,
are laughing at the stars. He hiked with a shepherd's crook and

led me to mariposa lilies, to ruins along volcanic saddles, to rings
of saguaro fruit we picked with clumsy poles. The ruins nestled in

the rocky hills that ring the valley must have been a lonely, sleepless
promontory. One tired eye was always on the water. Here the dead

enter a world choked in old mesquite: sooty survivors, roots touching
hundreds of rocky feet, touch caliche. Touch the water table.

III.

*Open the dam, flood the river valley, float for us a resort, we want
an arena, we want a riverboat rez casino. We want the Lucky Belle.*

The O'odham trekked across the Sonoran Desert to gather
salt from the gulf. A people without lakes, rivers, or brooks,

prayed and waded into the waves. The drive-through lube
is a hole in the ground the car rolls over, and the man with

the grease gun dreams about worker's compensation.
In the bottlebrush, a mockingbird turns an eye to me

and opens its beak. I've forgotten what I wanted to say. A line
of cars stretches from Baseline Road to the Sea of Cortez,

and most have no reason to gather salt. Nothing to tell
the sea foam. And when I hear my name out loud

for the first time in weeks, I am given an air filter.
Wheels and axles, a world of lubricants and belts,

the surgeon forgets my name; the nurse shaves and
marks the correct leg. In a stranger's hands I fall

asleep and drop my keys. He may keep them. The flash
flood finds us. When it ends and leaves us with

sunlight over the resorts and avenues, the stranded cars
shimmer in the current—coins in a well.

IV.

Northern, soothsayer skies. Black Mesa coal is burning,
pushing water uphill to trickle through the circuits of Phoenix.

66 pounds per cubic foot, roots probing the calcite depths,
mass of weighty thorns, the ironwood is still related to the pea.

No one is running to the mission to pray inside the adobe walls;
the weathered Jesuit bone settles in the scrub and dirt.

The neighborhood sleeps on hot pavement. Searchlights badger
a rock named Praying Monk. One climber falls; another holds

on. A storm jars me from sleep, and curtains of dust take
the White Tank Mountains from the horizon in one gulp.

3,000 gallons a minute. If you walk far enough and listen, water
will begin to prophesy in the liquefied slurry of crushed coal.

Rolling blackouts. What haven't we bent to our will? A storm is
spreading like oil, and power lines beget power lines beget power...

V.

Only some of the story is hidden: the old irrigation buried
beneath sewers and avenues poke through the dirt. Phoenix keeps

pace with its skeleton. She is trying to hide on Indian School Road
late at night with a wet towel on her head, and she dreams of ether

and a good sleep on the bottom of a canal. How did we get here?
The teeth of the spillway are full of tricycles. Red lights

shoo aircraft away from South Mountain. On-ramps lead
to dusty oblivion. Take me to where you were born, the arroyo

turned orchard turned office space. They have started the
foundation. Bring a blanket. We'll descend into the hole

and floodlights. The wilted man in the parking booth takes
my money, lets me out of the structure. When we drive,

we obey. Horizons scatter— we obey. I've been reading the birds:
a trio of Harris' hawks hunt the lap dog. A turkey vulture

heaves a sigh in the violet tufts of jacaranda trees in the gated
community. Old creases emerge in the desert floor.

The plane pushes through a dust storm, the swimming pools,
hollow stones set in the temple door. All night, lanes converge.

LOST AUBADE

Once it was my business
to know what lovers say when the sun
disturbs their lovemaking,

but alone, my hands long emptied
and you away, in a sketch
forever crossing your legs astride a horse,

I must walk with a small light that holds me,
the wall's cold hands and child's watercolor
of a buffalo cooling soup she spoon-feeds

her young. Please tell me
again the story she tells her daughter.
Your photographs of figurehead maidens

comfort no one. Underway
no sailor could see the low-bodiced girls
with oceanic eyes, and on Isla Negra,

you and I could rise early
and gather like shells the flotsam
of ships, the wooden girls

Neruda was so fond of. But shadows
scurry across glass faces, and I can't tell
prayer from elegy, the praying heart

from demands for pleasure.
A small chain of summer storms
darkens your room, the screen now blank—

a medicine cabinet emptied
of all its bad habits. I've lost
a morning song in the middle of the night.

I rise from the desk to windows
flickering with branches, all marrow
giving in, severing and falling

like caught voyeurs through leaves,
and although I lift a match to my face,
what new isolation is ushered in

by my reflection in picture frames? Beyond
a weary-eyed figure, is something
salvaged, empty-handed, oddly wooden

and sea-worn in the glass? What world
could I illuminate, what hoped-for good
asked for by the heart, and then hushed.

PARABLE OF THE SPARROW

In the casino, a brief union of face cards,
miracle of grapefruit, of vodka and quivering

plastic fern against a vent, the flower
of the dealer's cummerbund fades as he smokes

on break and gathers again as if nothing had
ever happened. Infrangible and lithe,

a keeper of time and games, he wants the bird
away from the table, outside where the equinox

is always spent, where non-artificial light
translates into another long journey toward

a patch of ice under an overpass, yet more winter
of court dates and mattresses on the floor, but like leaven

lost sheep, wheat, weeds, bridesmaids, brides, lost
coins and sons, the sparrow

in your hands is here to question, and unlike allegory
in which every part of the story

means something, here you take what you can
as double doors open wide to parking lots.

You must show the players brothering you
that the water of the sparrow's eye might

hold heroic weight, for you want to walk
upon it, but the vacuous

world of the eye inside your hands,
no source or sun behind it, offers only

the terror you temporarily hold. This hand
is irrevocable. Closing in, you are whispering

into cupped palms what you have been telling
strangers for years: *Our lives, you and I, are growing smaller,*

and like a fire you once built on ice,
the sparrow longs to vanish.

STATE OF THE UNION

How to translate, if I were
a dead Spanish poet, snow light
falling on this town, red-incarnadine,

flesh-colored, impossible ink from some
sea animal turning through
curtains, through newly landscaped trees

of the way things are, so that
we could know the barred windows
of the apartment complex, baby aspens

planted by property managers
so late in the season they will die.
Wires and cages built to

hold them will stay along the road
named Anasazi, like waymarkers
in some prophetic book

back when there was such a thing as *exile*.
Exile, the eye in the side of the bird
you have been gazing into all night,

astonished that it could weather
the freakish cold, is not your
eye, and this somehow helps,

but look again
and it's the polished lace ring
of a boot, the pair of which

someone slipped off
and threw onto a power line.
And stopped walking. So angry, could you

throw yourself headlong into
some bed or town? Even
this one. And I couldn't distinguish

one rented horn from a gymnasium
of children playing the banner—
a song about the body—

but it didn't matter,
I stood still, fancied
the sails and rudder,

darkly O darkly
on shallow water
of the desert city,

my polar star,
music so faintly
stretched, it didn't matter

stretched so faintly
it didn't matter.
Eye-ring to the trees

the spirit does not
give you its creature eye,
muck and twine, current

pushing you, the hands of a clock,
brittle reed, lesser
coverts, barring, under-

wing coverts, press your
head against the shell that carries you,
smear of light. You will be

the groom. You will be
the bridegroom—brief
confusing music that you are.

Looking for Federico

Parque Federico García Lorca, Granada

If a gray mare were here to lower her head
into the arms of a wounded rider,
and if from some distant promontory
officers of the Guardia Civil were raising
binoculars to stone faces, and if you
found yourself privy to a young man
weeping into his hat, you would
be either in the world of elegy
or among the curios they sell at the gate,
each plate a shimmering cliché of the poet
smiling in a plaza or playing piano for Dalí,
Romance Sonámbulo's refrain in gold
across a cigarette lighter, sixty wounded riders
loving the green, but in the center, the house
is a wind-polished bone one could overlook
for the roses that crowd the paths
and well-tended rosemary. People stroll
on the gravel after a siesta, yawning,
answering tiny phones in their coats.
From the poet's doorstep you follow
them in their circles as if they were workers
grinding a mill—these citizens content
to turn left or right until the light narrows
and they must leave. You may search
the wrought iron if you want. Is there a trace,
a *duende* of circumstance? A boy
is planting bougainvillea, and as he
turns the thorny strands, the lavender
blossoms begin waving to you
like the gloved hands of children.

After Mistranslating Del Camino XXII

Inside desire, Antonio
Machado, paths
are tangled,

can't be trusted,
but we travel
as the pony's bright fly

ends a majestic life adrift
in the folds
of night flowers. Black gates

of the park pitch
shadows at the calm.
I can't tell memory

from bauble,
stars from destiny.
I recognize the pilgrim

insofar as he
travels in the shadow
of a spent old man.

There's a fragrant turn
in the road,
the terrible taking

its course,
maybe half goat—horns strung
with roses, set in stubborn

motion,
and far off broods
a dispute

in the mind,
a finger of smoke
in olive groves.

ANTONIO MACHADO AND THE TREES

Baeza 1915

The poet is eavesdropping on the sycamores
at dusk. They talk with the copper light, the wind
they trap with long, knotted fingers—
their shapes racing against the chipped walls
of the village where he has banished himself at forty
to live with his mother, now that his child bride
has been two years in the grave. In the light
and chatter of the trees, the poet is resolved
to die teaching children French,
to live out what's left, years shipwrecked in a sea
of smoldering olive groves, the small pleasures
of regular verbs and nightfall in rural Spain.
He has only to read the gossip of the trees,
their talk of the lost bride. *Leanor*, they say, how fragile
she was when they married, and how consumption
riddled her away from him. The sycamores know
there was so little left of her that he secretly wanted
to carry her coffin like a guitar case
against his chest, with neither company nor ceremony,
all the way to the grave. As the day fades, the trees
mutter in their ranks before the last light leaves them.
The conversation is over. The poet, ashamed,
exposed on his hill, shivers
among the silent arches, the dark plaza,
where lions bite down on the brass rings of the doors.

Borges Falling Down the Stairs

National Library, Buenos Aires, 1969

Destiny has its way
    with Borges, cruel symmetry in repetition
        to forever elaborate useless ways,
            all the way
        to the bottom of the cellar. This is
    a pure diversion of my will, a way
through laborious cosmology, to exult
    in yet another circular solitude.
        The ineffable core is always solitude,
            illusion of pain in mirrors, the way
        the ceaseless stairs offer but a slight change in the series
    now and then, a sharp turn in the well, the series

resumed, some feeble artifice of Borges lost in a series
    in a wool suit, way-
        ward limbs straining toward the repetition—
            to halt the spectral series
        of collisions, the stairs and Borges,
    to forever elaborate the series
of jars and pitching dramas, a series
    within series of death and a rethinking
        of history's landfill of metaphors. Stop
            thinking and the stairwell may come to an end; think,
    and the steps stretch toward oblivion, your solitude
complete. The core is always solitude, always, always

Borges falls. What does Borges fall to?—some perfection
    of a series
        created by the world it bounds, a dizzying idiosyncrasy
            no doubt—the only place where all places are, solitude
        seen from every angle without overlap with each way

exulting in another,
Borges falls toward Borges, who, in falling solitude
    takes the shape of a man pointing in ecstasy
        both to heaven and to earth, a spiraling
            gesture showing the lower world's dark solitude
        is the map and mirror of the higher. The thinking
    Borges moves toward the *tornada* inside a thinking

and signifying Aleph, whose thinking
    conjures all stars, all lamps, pure ecstasy
        without confusion begetting
            stars, minerals, plants, every series,
        mutation, every secret and property, thinking
    no more stairs, no more stairs, Borges—but
alkali flats, planes, pampa, a single mattress, a way
    out of this Shih Hwang Ti of stairs, a short way
        to the bottom of this cycle,
    some two bit fruit of delirium, some ecstatic

grackle numb on berries is no delirious ecstasy
    as it flies into a mirror image. I have become
        the letters in a closed book, an ecstasy
            of iotas and dots, the characters lost in
        happenstance, but the stories gather in the solitude
    of the binding, and they keep Borges falling
as one in vertigo, oneiric tigers bounding in ecstatic
    talk down the well. This series
        of forking rivulets, eternal and tied series
            of actual and ersatz stars,
    that a nearby accordion might
    grind its way into the labyrinth of Borges' ear, O be
done with me.

roil (roil), *v.t.* [[rust, robigo, akin to French *ROUILLER, RUBER, RED*]] **1.** To render (water, wine, etc.) turbid by stirring up sediment. —SYN. ANNOY, FRET, RUFFLE, EXASPERATE, PROVOKE, RILE, VEX: *to be roiled by delay* [?]— **2.** *v.i.* to be agitated. **3.** *v.t.* To make (a house) cloudy, muddy, or unsettled by stirring: *The storm blew open the doors and roiled the house.* **4.** FIG. To render (a house, household, family, etc.) cloudy, muddy, or unsettled with an intent to annoy, fret, ruffle, exasperate, provoke. *The drunk father blew in from Mexico and roiled the house with the unexpected storm.*

roil² (roil), *v.t.* **1.** To gather (child, clothes, keys) and flee. **2.** (AMERICANISM) to disturb or disquiet; irritate; vex (neighbors) by screaming in the front yard of a house. *The father and mother roiled the neighbors shortly before dawn.*

roil³ (roil), *v.t.* **1.** To move (child, self, clothes) to a trailer home in a canyon by a creek. **2.** (AMERICANISM) To fire bottle rockets into a creak or stream. **3.** *-adj. ICHTH.* Characterized by being fired upon by a bottle rocket. *The roiled trout suffered a case of the nerves.*

roil⁴ (roil), *v.i.* **1.** To fall off a cliff in San Carlos, Mexico. **2.** To wake up in a Guaymas hospital with a head shaved and stitched up like a baseball. **3.** To wake up in a Guaymas hospital convinced that nuns singing in the dark are two tents on a camping trip where one's absent family is having a good time. **4.** (AMERICANISM) To regret. **5.** [NOW RARE] To repent. *In the hospital bed and darkness of the nun's hymn, his father roiled.*

Two Letters

(The Poet and Photographer)

Dear Mark, there is
a wash of peach
light that might

be the flower girl's breast
or the firm hemispheres
of a swimmer's back, and

I recognize the delicate
and petaled shadows
gathering leaf-like as…

what's the use? You could have
taken this picture
through a sandwich bag

or from space. Somehow
you have rigged your Nikon
to an electron microscope.

Forgive me, but is this
a picture of your lover
or the magnified surface

of an egg?
Your friend and poet,
Miles.

Enclosure

Dear Miles— Thanks
for your honesty
and poem, "Midnight Snack

with Lorca," but as much
as I enjoy the skull
in the ewe's milk,
the harlequin cats
going at it
in the walls, and even
your hidden monks
arming themselves
in the pharmacy—
the monozygotic moon
and hobbled pony
in the rosemary
throw me
for a loop.
The lavender gloved boys
are neither menacing
nor visceral,
and that's no way
to describe a flower
in the wind.

      Munch crackers
in moonlight
with some other martyr
for a change.
I'd be happy
to show you
what bougainvillea
looks like.
Yours,
Mark.

MÁLAGA

Nothing left to blink with, heads on, yet staring at us in
crowns or ringlets, tails hooked to lapdog teeth, fish on
platters waiters hurry to us, plaza giving way to loading
cranes that promise ocean—never delivering beyond a low
cover of palms, lashes swimming in medians the city has
lowered them into, watchers abound and are riddled in cliffs,
in far away caves, outskirts, invitations to talk of lives we
will never lead. Must we admit, over our small table of bones
that we dreamed once of eschewing this life, that the window
to run away had shut long ago? —though dashlights of
our cab ride, filthy dusk, and radio signal have silenced us,
distant ships and strollers seem to sway a bit beneath the old
wires that were once *fuegos artificiales.* The neckties of
Málaga are loosened. Carving keys in shops no bigger than
what delivers us to the edge, are tired men, and a flurry
of woodwinds compels our driver to warn us that when
the mermaid rises from the ruined river to walk into this life,
he will protect her from us, *mariquitas.* No, we don't
remember the carousel that turned on Sundays, how the
waters would leave you and appear again, flute cadenza cutting
up the transmarine waves fish look to be rising into, grinning
sockets, eyes mere memory, wooden horses in a warehouse
fire we cannot see, driver please turn the dial, his finger we
now follow to a patch of water where a pier had been.

DUST STORM

The clouds
        are claiming
what the piano teacher

        asked you to repeat last week
small sounds
        you must find again

among many
        arpeggios maybe
that should leap

        from the lacquer
on cue but you have
        only the instrument

vast and foreign
        before you
alkali flats the faces

        of student and teacher
must float in
        you wait there

on the bench
        until her fingers
find dark keys.

        You listen carefully
to the angry cinnamon
        gallop of gum

in her mouth and
            precision of nails on tiles
blood shooting in your ears.

            The wind is
trying to lift
            the house again

loose ends like trash
            or even tiles
head skyward and you

            would very much
like to be a plastic bag
            above trees.

Motes hang
            before windows
waiting for you

            on the stand
is sheet music
            you don't understand—

your turn
            to fidget again
and try to parrot

            what you have heard
but the ants
            are caged inside

the abacus
        and muted hammers
aren't falling for you.

        The storm
dazzling a bush
        flats and sharps

slip into drapes
        into the body
of a sleeping dog.

DOGS

Within range of chain or through slats
we gaze at the blades of the shepherd's ears
and stupidly think wolves.
        We marvel at dream-chases
that send them kicking in their sleep.
Let us eat out of their mouths
they are so clean. So noble
and loyal they protect the family
that abandons them in a parking lot,

and the master too, who once
untethered them as he worked
on an automobile must
be protected, his memory
burning in their small, perpetually
prejudiced skulls,
        and that's why
we love them:
        they bring the _____ out in us.

On criminals and a world that hurts us
we let them loose with a handful
of utterances to which we pin
meaning, and if they are good
they come back to us
with strange balls or toads,

a mouth full of quills, or
they find a stranger, a pedestrian,
suspiciously slogging along, and come
what hell there will be company
in a public walk, their flews and whithers,
bristled rump, quivering
stifles and pasterns, every
celebrated inch of them bred
for the stranger: me.

39

LOVER OF SNAKES

For weeks I've been trying to reach
the lover of rattlesnakes,
monkey grass, mariposa lilies
in the rocky basalt above the canyon,
packrats in the yucca outside his cabin,
jojoba —more nutlike & bitter than berry—,
the zone tailed hawk as much
as the turkey vulture it copies,
the zopilote nest he found
in northern Mexico, saguaro fruit
we picked with poles we stole
from land surveyors, lichen, elf owls, moss,
what's left of the humpback chub,
the desert five spot, a small spring I swore
I would show no one (where blackberries
and a diamondback thrived) catclaw
acacia, creosote, ant lions, the tarantula
that paid us no mind in the trail,
gnat catchers, Harris' hawks he hoped
no falconer would tame, mesquite,
bark scorpions, the jeweled and docile
gila monster's slow and secretive ways,
scrub oak,
          words—precise as coyote scat
full of berries and prickly pear (thorns and all)—
atop a pile of stones,
the small coyote we saw leap
from a juniper branch in the middle of a storm
(the air around us—rich with ions, lightning, and lusty plants—
was delicious, he said),
          and Madrecita, little mother,
Earth—to whom we say aloud,
thank you.

Yard

Along the arroyo, there is no liveliness, no force
beyond a mere and oracular flat, well-tended and

without wind or similes in trees. No angels. How to be
not right with a creator, but honest? A plane is

not going down with specified mercies. For those who dance
tonight on public access television, much must mean

nothing but dancing convincingly. I have changed channels
all night to come to this—dawn, cold and closer than wanted,

and to the conviction that the Rattlesnake River is
named after what people rarely see. Take the parakeet

grave and time capsule my mother and I buried, a gold
book about the ark, a sandwich and toy soldier crawling

upon whatever world we put beneath him—cigar box
among palm tree roots, sprinkler heads. Sagging ditch-ward a stone

wall divides and chips away in topsoil the arroyo
takes someplace. The more we pour into it, the more it will

carry away the yard—vatic, vapid. Did he notice
this on the morning before his surgery, my father

lingering in this narrow light? The eyes clutching the not-so-
fine mist sprinklers heave upon the lawn are my own. Now yours.

QUAIL

Dusk is swollen with old stories and behind the wheel
there is no remembering them. Sensors trick on
halogen lights. You leave your car
along the interstate and shuffle off the bright shoulder
into the arroyo where summer is over and cicadas
are sleeping, where the wellspring of coyote laughter—
sudden and kindred—sinks in. In the brambly watershed,

white thorn acacia and silence hold you with nettled hands.
Mesquite tufts fork, crack like alkali flats
against the sky. A feather bush is still and dark.
From hummingbird trumpet, a sphinx moth twitches away,
and the night's distant fluttering is like sea water
flooding the workings of your father's watch, or as when he called
out to you from a lone ironwood tree

and you rose from an uneasy sleep to run barefoot
and terrified to his voice. Inside the thorny mass, his hands
held a buff-collared nightjar tangled in the branches.
His fingers beneath the flashlight spread the dead-leaf patterns
of a wing. *This*, he said, *is a mystery.* He bloodied
his wrists to free it from the thorns— where tonight you find
yourself pushing through brambles to a house,

hollow and beached in its yard. The last of the powder light
ripens around weathered riggings, and beyond the gate,
a cluster of trees you cannot name compels you to enter
their world of murmuring birds. Each tree a family,
a hemisphere of dozing quail. At your step,
into rivulets of stars, umbral boughs,
and startled wings, they scatter.

Equuleus

Moonrise, Wukoki, 1999

Without garden they woke to impulse, were
poorly suited to surfaces that shunned

their strides. If it was cold, they exhaled storms,
if it hailed on them, they stormed back cutting

themselves, cutting in half the night they let
pass beneath their gait, only to join it

again transformed, no less inhospitable
as any underworld of our making,

thunder cells of first steps retold in the
painted skies of their skin. Saddled without

rider, moonrise blinding Cassiopeia's
Chair before another turn, we say now

that the horse followed us to the ruins,
that crater-scarred worlds shifting in haunches

as she walked were ours, that four winged fruits, wing-
like bracts of saltbush, were radiant

as if she knew what we in our telling
never arrive at. We lay where roofless

walls opened to the sky, where the dead were
buried in floors, perhaps the bones of a

child holding us in place, row upon row
of stones ending in stars. She had come so

far, this mare who lowered her head into
fields of one-seeded fruits that do not split.

Winds went on sharpening rock back to earth.
As if waking for the first time into

our lives, we were luminous, honed with her,
and into this world, we woke as strangers.

REUNION

Farther we go the more
we bury them
and misunderstand each

other sitting with our
cups on the brink of another
commemoration—the meat

gets smaller on the grill
smaller still the tree
winds eat when they

pick up on this stretch
of lawn where we've
been remembering

in loud voices how
we will make changes
soon the sea far beyond

the mountain haze-hidden
lost thought sleepers
somewhat owl song

how we would like
to find whomever—our
selves someday a place

in it and know
be sure of what
we wanted heard.

FIRE EATER

Into a body
mostly water
and a humming
light inside
the bulb, over-
head, holding
a ringing note,
an anonymous
horn down a
canal, the inner-
ear —but here
is only out-
side spinning
its captured ball
with the far reaching
legs and spindled
torque of the venomous.
                  Tell me
how long have I
been living on
this interstate
overpass, whose
cars and freight
speeding below
behave as though
they've had no
light in years?
This can't be,
rending time
from the coal.
I exhale
and grotesques

who animal or
people the city
are humiliated
by their names:
adult boutiques
called Paradise,
a horse track
named Turf
Paradise,
churches, motels,
Desert Wind,
The Dunes, Amigos
en Algo, the Grotto.
Don't cling
to any of these
ideas passing for
traffic as if
the air filled
suddenly with inroads
and unlucky moths
were as soft
as doves and didn't
burn… What is
that song, that
horn I would
gladly fall to,
glittering glass
of accidents? Can I
stay here, mere
rising in the corner
of your eye
as you drive,

the response
I commit
myself to? Can we,
after the body, go on
startling awake?
Is this our
absence illuminated—
a hum slowed
to a knell,
and from such
heights and tongues.

Dust Devil

Enough to press against me a child's buried voice of grain
blown would enter me would

pull out light braids would flick blouse and skirt enough to
summon arms' weight would grant you quick

aridity you would
                              on the seams of sudden
gathering like omen or would-be weather

dance if I would only stay awhile beyond fleeing
ground and keep you beyond chain link

stay within the flame holding me still
let me go maker earth a flame of me world blurring from

which I would never part
                                        spinner ephemera that
chooses me since I am dreamer enough to conceive what conceives
me scattered making for others

a sudden confusion of field a sudden unraveling detritus

mere turn among many beyond your fragile reach and

beyond are you threatened or saved beyond dreaming
runners catching limina are nearly spent your

blooming orrery too many worlds would
be tangled to you beyond any

reach now happenstance treaded enough
for dirt and incompatible enough

for you my dizzying eye beyond a blink less sudden
than what touches you suddenly union

fleeing brief steps sudden beyond which you are
must be as any reflected conception falling would

be less would suddenly not be enough.

DRINKING IN THE DAYTIME

The day is submersed in oil, viscous copper, a distortion
that buckles the air, men's room and old piano

that is locked but you can look at it and hear
someone coughing, someone saying

Sober up all you want, no one is going anywhere.
Tengo sueño, a girl says. Sleepy, she is

either dreaming or bored with him, and
soon, her heels are firing

away from us into the street, out to workers
in their holes, to their laughter and laying

of fiber optics. One failure usurps another
like mandibles missing teeth in the vacant skulls

above us grimacing among
our chrome reflections and a local

news story about thirst and heatstroke.
And hidden in our rapt expressions, there is

the conviction that nothing can keep us
from swimming to the surface of this place and rising

through a pressed tin ceiling
into some lake world we have been dreaming about

where dimly lit cabins along the shore harbor
other lives, where we are up to our necks

in a voyeur's warm water and gazing into
far away rooms, and we can leave

the agitated fire inside the glass words,
CERVEZA ESPECIAL

and leave the orifice of the puma's skull, the cracked
sobs of the man three stools down,

the rubber grapes, socketless, fathering only dust,
the bottles saying Crème de Cacao and Blue Curaçao,

the x-ray of someone swallowing water on the screen
with laboring tongue, whose bones

are no more important than gossamer or smoke
or the old man wandering into the yucca. The young man

is splashing cold water on his face.
Mirrors brighten inside his body.

Sleepers

Cottonwoods, strong and mortal,
shimmer in the commons, and although
the men I have killed myself with
lower their beards to the coin-
scarred bar, waking up
in jail or love or here in the library.
I can hear the wooden dolls the roots
of trees will make breathing
stories for the world beneath
parking stripes and man
dreaming in the cool of the library,
his shirt a crumpled ball
beneath his head that is my head,
and some afternoons the closest
I can come to loving the world
is loving the same three words
yelled along the elbow
of a river where caddis flies
thicken the light, where there is
no one, no stacks, no hum
of nuclear clock, mercurial
gurgle of Miro's sundial
in Barcelona, as if the words
beading across the world's surface *I
am here I am here*
were my story, my prayer.

Against Querencia

If there was land in the heart's reliquary,
watershed or canyon, arsenic dredge

and spent mine, there was also my pickup
parked at the foot of a crumbling rise, a halo

of light behind it promising Mexico.
In the truck cab, behind frosted windows, a dream kept me

climbing a butte whose shadow fell on either Mexico
or Arizona—Nogales more or less—depending on

whether the moon was strong enough to throw
a weaker form of rock, south or north…

But waiting at the top in shale and bottle shards,
was my self, maybe ten, shivering, gazing

into lights of another country, and I had to rise
to a task just beyond the body, a false

return to what had never happened,
climbing a hill near a border so beleaguered

by crossing and patrol its desert had become a trumped up
replica of itself: succulents, islands in a sea of tracks.

I climbed all night to find the child tired of waiting—
would we make Hermosillo by dawn? Old man—

are you going to leave me here? And soon,
boasting at lights in the hills—*Upon killing a bird*

that mates for life they founded a city, and I was born—
but out there with no one awake

to witness, one window glowed in an old hotel, a bulb
faceless behind a grate, an empty elevator anonymous

as a man climbing a hill, stumbling upon
himself as a child who keeps asking him questions

from the silt of alluvium—*Why don't we*—and he had my voice—
take our father out of the caves?

And after fire devoured Las Cavernas Cantina, blackened
rock walls, they bricked in the mouth of the cave. I stop sweeping

the cafeteria floor to remember this and to write
the words: *faraway comparisons*, or do I write *companions*?

Pictures, a plastic Mayan calendar, velvet curtains
cleared away. Children pick up instruments,

and in the bad acoustics of a gymnasium, the band
begins to play a Sousa march, slowly, poorly,

two four time running into the tiles. Bleachers creak
beneath the weight, the melody stitched

together by a snare. If there must be music, there
must also be heat rising from asphalt and lawns, holding a bird

whose only partner is fire. Late, by flashlight
through the empty school, paper bodies

rise in classroom windows. By a small fire
in the playground, blue and yellow bars racing with shadows,

the face that appears in the embers belongs to no one
and is tasting something bitter. Its mouth opens, and I speak

names into the coals and wait. Some nights
the sky is like a blue shell stolen

from a missionary's tomb, cupped to my ear so that
I can hear far off waves and voices, swifts otherworldly

and whistling through the narrows
of what was never there.

Harvest

As my father died, he tended to his obsessions.
I found him in the garden instead of bed.
Shooting gophers, he'd stand in slippers, blue
checkered robe, 16-gauge low on the shoulder,
a Burpee seed catalogue pressed under an arm.
He dragged the drooling desert hose to the peas
and forgot to take pills, or at night when the beat

of his slippers troubled him, when the dog
moved its slow collar along the tile, when it couldn't
lick what stung, fire arrived at my window.

As my father died, he let the thrush pick the cat,
and the dog's arthritic hip worked through the bleak
afternoon doorways, the side of the house
where the bottlebrush bloomed outside my room,
and the wasps had attached a nest beneath the roof.
They had a field day on the dog's hide
and made it twitch. God knows why

my father died. As my father died, he touched a torch
to the eaves where wasps had built a city of drifting
anger, where late on a school night, I put a face
to the red pane and watched their quick wings

turn on them like angels made of hair
slow to find the ground. The side of my father's
checkered face was held in a light I thought
set aside for the lighting of candles.
Not the hive girdled in flames. Not the strange flower.

Tavern Song

We were born into this world
To kill time, to marvel at the bird
Lighting across the doorway,

None of us certain what it will bring
Back in its beak, nor where to,
But the room is underway,

And though the jukebox
Was taken from us,
We bring flowers to the owner

And cry into his hands,
And here is where I've begun again
To write my prayer and number

Above the urinal…and here
I have written her name, and if I have
Kissed my hand walking in,

I only wanted salt—look, even the door
Divorced from hinges regrets
And faces the wall in padlock coils,

And here is the man next to me
With photographs of daughter and home
Taped to his hand grenade lighter, and here—dream apple,

Power broker in halter top and freckled shoulder,
Is the bartender, who has sculpted
An effigy of me in modeling clay:

Honored, I hold a coin half my size,
With the other, I hold my genitals.
Look into my mouth—a hole,

Burrowing through the back of the head—
One can see neon, and the tanned
Hides of shipwrecked checks

And the words *be good*
Lovingly tacked on tongue-in-groove lumber.
Look again and all of us, hatchlings,

Open our beaks,
The scorpion loose inside the nest—
No matter, world or stranger, put

Your ears to my lips.
Sing through me,
And the song will be repeated.

Sleepers II

Said goddamn me
instead of bless me
and am not sure why

must speak more
of me than what
I'd wish for

for anyone
but I remember him
the father singing

my head against
his great belly
the lights

go so far
away in our window
we wonder together

who might live there
and sing
in the softness

our dinner on our breaths
rock of rocking chair
traveling.

HARP

Whatever the harp may tell us in dry night air where we have been
>   told not to stray
from the familiar circles street lights cast and trees which must be
>   paloverdes but
may be Chinese somethings lining cul-de-sacs—asses of bags in
>   French—streets
like turned goblets when we are on our mother's roof to watch
>   something distant
burn long enough for an old car whose smoke ascends above
>   the valley to shape
a graceless bird tinted blue reflecting lights though it may promise
>   flight egress etc.,
soon the catastrophe is cleared and we are left facing a small radio
>   and antennae whose
discordant echoes are for a much younger audience—be quiet
>   watch your step
they are sleeping under us stay still *quédate quieto*—it is far more
>   architecture than
instrument the harp excepting the campanile and to linger in
>   the firmament of light
pollution or to look down upon hummingbird feeders and
>   bougainvillea blossoms'
lavender sailing across a shallow end of a shadowy pool is to
>   suddenly think
tabernacle—dear heart if I were more penitent—swelling lamps
>   eyes and wings are

drawn to don't mother me perhaps I was frightened in a storm
      when I first
tasted it—where would I be?—to look down from rooftops
      and to listen to
antiquated flurries both harp and radio waves have brought us
      is to think again of
a home we will not readily leave of how all of our so-be-its have
      brought us this
far: to our whistle our dark.

Swimmers

3.

Faces of trigger fish
are not our faces. They are
faces born as arrows,

glass-eyed trajectories
now in heaps upon the deck—
one fish turns itself

over in the air: another eye—
nearly another
fish, and the father's

one good eye bids us
clean these changelings
pumping nothing in the sunlight,

a day's sail from nowhere,
near a rock in the Sea of Cortez
named Monserrat, the boat

adrift, drawing slowly as a blade
in the alien air.

2.

The eight ball touches
nothing on its way to the hole.
On this piece of paper, you have

begun to answer the counselor who brings
you your shallow cup and pen.
Write for me—he reminds you—

and this is not a test—*ten things*
you value most. Priorities
he calls them, stars you cannot

see from here, that cannot leave
their obligations, even as two brothers—
in the back of a pickup driven

by a drunk father—gaze at them:
tack holes, lost and random
that when connected are called: bottles

rolling back to us on turns,
headlights from oncoming freight.
Hercules, Scorpius, Crux. I was

afraid. Add that fear to the list,
add the dog that dug beneath
the chicken wire into summer

squash, add that morning my brother
ran with the animal in his arms
to hide it from the ax, the father

behind the ax who made me
fetch a switch for my brother,
the eucalyptus I climbed into,

into whose branches I hoped to vanish.
I consider the sky
a priority I climbed. I thought

the Phoenix sky would make everything
a dream, something I could
later be grateful for, but the world

only grew sharper: the swamp cooler
rattle, doves in the leaves,
windows and brick behind which

I knew he had the dog, he had
my brother. And you are falling—
but not far onto a sandy shelf

inside a mine you do not
know, another clearing
of dust and light.

1.

You have shot a thousand rattlesnakes
whose heads now float in baby jars.
So that we may see their eyes.

You have shot my share
of mid-gaze mockingbirds
to be here. Beneath a patch of earth

that gives way, my brother's fingers

bridging a pool cue the day he took
one thousand dollars the recruiter

gave him and abandoned
boot camp in Oklahoma. He wanted
to see the ocean and kept saying

today had been the greatest of days.
On the lam, he said, *you notice
everything.* And come San Bernadino,

attention ran out.
He had hoped to throw himself
into the water, to keep going,

but confessed he would, at best,
throw his hemostats into the waves
before turning himself in,

but when he left them
hanging like gut from elk antler
I shot the game out alone,

taking my time on the eight,
thinking of weak stars in the west,
dawn exploding in my brother's mirror,

in the glass of trucks, in the bottles—the chiming
Indonesian parade he carried inside him.
Exhausting itself beyond mile markers,

Quonset huts were burning in alfalfa
fields at dawn, and from the sway
of dust and spores, this man,

a red faced card, is speaking over
his shoulder in a jack's regalia,
his one good eye commanding you

to swallow the fish at the bottom of the cup
that are sometimes there, and at other times—
in the hum of the ward—hard to find,

where the brother beside you in a sleeping bag
must circulate a bulwark of chemicals to keep
the silence of the cards in his hands.

O.

As you slip into the air, add fiberglass,
and oxygen, add the syllables
medication keeps, the bad news lithium

is gently breaking to you
over and over, you are throwing
weak circles and will not surface,

add this falling body, not even
a stranger's, add all that luxuriates in
inevitable absence.

SLEEPERS III

On pitched roofs, winter's weight between bricks, sunset leaves gilded
wisps, half the sky a storm, the week's only light— it seems so

late and halved in the day the visible holds weather that
might only happen to others, never here above yards,

frozen distances unraveling at the skirts of trees
we know are hiding rooms, what some

keeper left, never us we think, a
wind's note working thin

walls, many reed
instruments—

cells where
once bees

were
kept.

TIDES

After bedtime, the boy forgets something, a bike
left on its side in the scrub behind the yard, plastic soldiers

in the arroyo, lose ends that keep him up, sending him
into the desert to gather

the pieces in his pajamas and sneakers, and there,
beneath a degree of moon and shadow, he finds his father

moving a chair into the night on the property's edge,
a voice, the surrender of ice in bourbon, the ember

of a cigar in a shadow's hand. He continues

to forget and doesn't sleep, the chair
growing empty, the house fills with strangers

standing and covered dishes, dress shoes
striking the tiles, the minister's hand arrives,

the garden falls into itself, the water table
drops, mountains beyond the yard sprout transmitters,

horizons brown with homes and roads.

When the water leaves, what remains? The tide
will never come back in, and the moon moves through

an earth gone brittle beneath his feet, a desert
of seeds without edges, of fine powder, beneath tires,

that keeps the eyes from ever crying. He can hear
the television sets of his neighbors, radios behind car windows,

someone coughing in a kitchen. He is awake

beyond the yard and builds a basket with what dies:
a cowboy's barbed wire, the hair of a pony

struck by lightning, cottonwood root, his father's
leather belt, creosote, Christmas lights

pulled from the tree, a hip bone that plagued
a German shepherd. From the debris

of a lost tide, he builds a basket and shoulders
it off the property.

NOTES

"Direction"

The Sinagua were prehistoric people of the northern region of
  Arizona who built sophisticated cave homes from 500 AD to
  1300 AD. They died out probably from disease, famine or
  drought.

"Phoenix Suites" was inspired by Charles Bowden's *Killing The
  Hidden Waters,* the University of Texas Press, 1977.

  I.

Hohokam were prehistoric people of the south-central Arizona
  desert 200 BC to 1450 AD. Some of their original irrigation
  canals are still being used in the Phoenix area. They traded
  with their neighbors the Anasazi and seem to have disappeared
  by the time the Spanish came upon their descendents.

  II.

The *saguaro* cactus grows to 50 feet and has been known to live
  100 years. Its arms do not appear until it is 75 years old.

Mesquite is among the most common shrub/small trees in the
  desert southwest. It restores nitrogen to the soil; its seedpods
  are used as food by humans, wildlife, and livestock, and its
  bark is used for basketry, fabrics and medicine.

Caliche is a hard layer of calcium carbonate formed just beneath
  the surface in arid places like Phoenix, which is caused by
  evaporation of rising solutions. These lime layers can be so
  tight that roots and water cannot penetrate them and growth
  is restricted leaving accumulations of salt on the soil surface.

  III.

O'odham, possibly descendents of the prehistoric Hohokam.

  V.

Section V. was inspired by Sherman Alexie's book *The Lone
  Ranger and Tonto Fistfight in Heaven*, Harper Perennial, 1993.

An *arroyo* is a dry gully. During wet seasons, it can be a temporary
  rivulet or stream.

"Lost Aubade" is for Meg Gannon and was inspired by Emily Dickinson's "The Heart asks Pleasure—first—" and Helen Vendler's discussion of the poem in *Poems, Poets, Poetry.* Bedford Books, 1997.

"State of the Union"
The Anasazi were cliff-dwellers of the southern Colorado Plateau and Northeastern Arizona, New Mexico and Utah.

"Looking for Federico"
Duende is a Spanish word which can mean ghost, spirit, or an enchanting quality, magic. Lorca wrote frequently of duende as a power of energetic instinct, mystery, which speaks through human creation. Lorca's celebrated poem "Romance Sonámbulo" contains the haunting refrain, "*Verde que te quiero verde* / Green how I love you green."

"Two Letters" is for Mark Hillis.

"Málaga" is for Jesús Cantudo Porcel.
Mariquita is a Spanish word literally meaning ladybug, but the taxi driver in the poem uses it as a derogatory term for gay men.

"Dogs" is for James Jay.

"Lover of Snakes" is in memory of Geoffrey Platts.
The *yucca* is also called "Spanish bayonet" for its big sharp leaves. From the center of the green spears grows a tall stalk bearing 15 greenish-white flowers.
Zopilote refers to either a black vulture or turkey vulture

"Yard"
Vatic: oracular or prophetic.

"Quail" is for John Walton Waggener.

"Equuleus" is a small northern constellation, The Little Horse, found between Delphinus and Aquarius.

"Dust Devil"

Limina is the threshold of a physiological or psychological response.

Orrery, a mechanical model of the solar system, is named after Charles Boyle (1676-1731), fourth Earl of Orrey, for whom one was made.

"Against Querencia"

Querencia is a loaded Spanish word meaning affection, fondness, homing instinct, den, lair, or roost. It can also refer to a home, a heart place. In bullfighting, it is the bull's favorite spot on the ring.

"Harp" is for Paul Tope.

Phoenix Suites is the winner of the 2002 Word Works Washington Prize. Miles Waggener's manuscript was selected from 453 manuscripts submitted by American poets.

FIRST READERS:
Nancy Allinson
Forestine Bynum
Donald Cunningham
Deanna D'Errico
Patricia Gray
Erich Hintze
James Hopkins
Tod Ibrahim
Mike McDermott
Kevin Pachas
Ann Rayburn
Maritza Rivera
Jill Tunick
Jonathan Vaile
Barry Wepman
Doug Wilkinson
Rhonda Williford

SECOND READERS:
J.H. Beall
Bernadette Geyer, *DIRECTOR*
Brandon Johnson

FINAL JUDGES:
Karren L. Alenier
Cynthia Hoffman
Miles David Moore
Martha Sanchez-Lowery, *DIRECTOR*
Hilary Tham

About the Author

Born and raised in Phoenix,
MILES WAGGENER currently lives
in Prescott, Arizona, where he
teaches writing at Prescott College.
Phoenix Suites is his first collection
of poetry.

Photo by Megan Gannon

About the Artist

MATT HAMON was born in San Francisco and grew up in rural
northern California. Matt graduated with a B.A. degree and a
teaching credential from Humboldt State University in California
and then went on to earn his M.F.A. from the University of
Washington in Seattle. He has taught photography at the
University of Washington and is currently pursuing his career in
photography and teaching at Prescott College in Prescott, Arizona.

About The Word Works

THE WORD WORKS, a nonprofit literary organization, publishes contemporary poetry in collectors' editions. Since 1981, the organization has sponsored the Washington Prize, a $1,500 award to an American poet. Monthly, Word Works presents free literary programs in the Chevy Chase Café Muse series, and each summer, free poetry programs are held at the historic Joaquin Miller Cabin in Washington, DC's Rock Creek Park. Annually, two high school students debut in the Miller Cabin Series as winners of the Young Poets Competition.

Since 1974, WORD WORKS programs have included: "In the Shadow of the Capitol," a symposium and archival project on the African-American intellectual community in segregated Washington, DC; the Gunston Arts Center Poetry Series (Ai, Carolyn Forché, Stanley Kunitz, among others); the Poet-Editor panel discussions at the Bethesda Writer's Center (John Hollander, Maurice English, Anthony Hecht, Josephine Jacobsen, and others); Poet's Jam, a multi-arts program series featuring poetry in performance; a poetry workshop at the Center for Creative Non-Violence (CCNV) shelter. Master Class workshops (Agha Shahid Ali, Thomas Lux, Marilyn Nelson) and the Arts Retreat in Tuscany are ongoing programs.

In 2003, WORD WORKS will have published 51 titles, including work from such authors as Deirdra Baldwin, J.H. Beall, Christopher Bursk, John Pauker, Edward Weismiller, and Mac Wellman. Currently, Word Works publishes occasional anthologies and books under three imprints: the Washington Prize, the Capital Collection and International Editions.

Past grants have been awarded by the National Endowment for the Arts, National Endowment for the Humanities, DC Commission on the Arts & Humanities, Witter Bynner Foundation, Writer's Center, Bell Atlantic, Batir Foundation, and others, including many generous private patrons.

THE WORD WORKS has established an archive of artistic and administrative materials in the Washington Writing Archive housed in the George Washington University Gelman Library.

Please enclose a self-addressed, stamped envelope with all inquiries.

WORD WORKS BOOKS